In Deep

In Deep

by

Maryna Ajaja

Wild Ocean Press
San Francisco

Thanks to the following publications in which some of these poems have appeared:

Raven Chronicles, Winter, 1996

Before There is Nowhere to Stand, Palestine/Israel: Poets Respond to the Struggle, an anthology, ed. Joan Dobie and Grace Beeler, Lost Horse Press, 2012

Also by Maryna Ajaja

Empatheia (chapbook), True Bug Press, 2013, designed and printed by Jenny Sapora

Book cover design by Solange Roberdeau

Book cover art, "Diver" by Marion Peck, used with permission of Debbie Lester, photograph by H. Friese

Ajaja, Maryna

In Deep

ISBN: 978-1-941137-12-3

Printed in the United States of America on 30% recycled paper

First edition

Distributed by Small Press Distribution, Inc., Berkeley, CA
http://www.spdbooks.org

Wild Ocean Press
San Francisco, CA
www.wildoceanpress.com

To Valeri Ajaja

Table of Contents

Part Four: Silence as a Crime

Part Five: Leeway

PART ONE

In Need of Random

Chimacum Cows

They arch their perfect backbones

          in the sun

               on the hillside,

    though massive clouds

            cross about

they face due east

     in perfect need of random,

           while the possibility of rain

    is sacred

        in some languages.

Overcoming Vertigo

I dream of a slab of volcanic rock

blocking the sun.

Others squat there too.

The sky darkens as the clouds build up.

Suddenly the slab breathes and a blowhole appears.

I feel hot breath and see electric green plankton.

I hold on in the storm though I'd like to let go

as I did before

in my green Dodge truck

on a high sheer icy winter road

despite having vertigo

or maybe just

to spite it.

LaConner

Low slung landscape.
Road above fallow cabbage.

Rich alluvial flat lands
where poets live and mourn the dead.

Daffodils in concession.
Row after row of confessions.

Night smell of bog and cow.
Small fires from the Reservation.

Tiny room, corner of town.
Farm country, male town.

Puer Aeternus

I follow the man in a green torn shirt
a bucket banging at his painter pant leg.
I can't tell what's in his bucket.
Raspberries, blackberries, or maybe a paint brush?
He strides like a nine-year-old.
It's hard to keep up with him.
Maybe I'll follow him for
the rest of my life and never see
inside his bucket.

Still Life on Hastings

A flat white house in a square field.
A pile of children's papers on a red chair.
A pile of papers in an off-white living room.
No starlight tonight but a red sky.
No streetlights but an orange moon.
Mom is on the back porch crying
thinking of dying.
Babies in the backroom sleeping
dreaming of waking
to a warm square house
with a picture window
and a pile of blank papers
on a red chair
in an off-white
living room.

Loveseat

After he throws the loveseat at me, I cannot get up. When he kicks
me in the thigh, the white socks, which I bleached clean, flash as his
jeans hike up. On the floor, the carpet is full of cracker crumbs. I
don't know how they got there—I just cleaned—but I inhale crumbs
and bits of dust and don't move. Above me, he lurches around like a
bear, tripping and bumping into corners with that glazed look of
forgetfulness, as if he doesn't know where he is. Unfortunately, I
know that look and I know where he is. Soon he'll wind down and
cry on my lap like a baby after a tantrum. I hate that loveseat he
heaved at me, passed down from my family. I guess I lack respect
for family jewels. It used to be upholstered in blue velvet and before
that it was flower brocade. Stuffed with horse hair, it's lighter than it
looks. I hate furniture and clutter. I'd rather live in a white empty
room. Rooms have sounds. Some sound hollow, others sound like
water in pipes or sizzling heaters, or vague fan sounds, or buzzing
electricity. Put furniture in a room and it gets in the way of the
sounds. My enormous father used to sit in that flowered loveseat.
He'd eat peanuts and watch football. He wore a crew-cut with black-
rimmed glasses and he would yell and hoot when something pleased
or displeased him and peanut spittle would fly from his mouth. He
hated kids. We kids avoided him though we had to pass through the
"family" room where he sat on that damn loveseat. Our mother was
great, though. She had a special whistle for us to find her at the mall.
She let us play dress-up and dance in the big room to *Oklahoma* and
South Pacific. Father hated mother because she tried to "better
herself." She went to college so she wasn't always at home and he
thought it was paramount that a woman be at home. How do we
start hating each other? A deep lesion festers and gnaws at the heart
valves. The selfless soul begins to selfishly keep track of the wrongs
as oceans of possibilities trickle down to puddles. At first you put on
your yellow rubber rain boots and slosh through, rain or shine,

taking some joy in the leaves and sky. But just as suddenly you are angry, your feet are wet, you have to clean up the mess, and you begin to mind the smell of their shit. After he had me down on the ground and did the things he did to me and was sorry, and after we sat at the table to eat our cold and wilted food and he vowed once more to never do it again, he went to bed. I have been good at waiting for him. But now I am through with fate. In the morning, I'll call Goodwill to pick up the loveseat, then pack.

Port Townsend

I walk to the store and buy a postcard of Venice.

The watery view of Port Townsend is clear.

The wind is crazy as a prairie woman.

Monet's gondola is out of line with the quay.

Everything here is lavender.

The ferry sidles in from Whidbey Island

its furious rudder plows foam.

I walk the one hundred thirty-eight steps past Galatea.

There are no people in the postcard.

Nothing keeps the viewer from the water.

Venice is a long way off.

PART TWO

Work of Mourning

...the grandchildren of the victims, perpetrators, and onlookers...
produce the work of mourning for their grandparents...

Alexander Etkind

Empatheia

If I could remove the stone from my mouth,
remove my mouth from my mouth,
my muscle of malcontent
so content deep in the folds
of my thyroid-less throat,
that butterfly-flat gland
of energy, personality and sex drive.
If I could remove the stone of ambiguity,
and lack of identity sitting
silent as a saint before supper.
If I could believe every day
was the last supper and there
would be no other chance to eat,
I would speak
and dedicate
this poem to you
in your last pouty sleep.

Everywhere I go I see you.
Your contradictions and unresolved afflictions.
Mommy, Mom, Mother, *mat*,
The Colonel, Grandma Plane,
Imelda with a thousand shoes.
Madame Alexander with glass eyes.

On Hastings a black cat crosses
in front of me from the left.
I had to spit twice, another stone on my precarious lips.
And I, most fearsome child,
hang upside down
in our oak in Van Nuys.

I'm not interested
in dolls with glass eyes.
Climbing rocks and bringing home bits of schist,
hunks of garnet in the matrix.

I was never your doll,
your plaything.
Resolute, persistent,
pigeon-toed in patent-leather shoes,
pinafore and ponytail
with Hopalong Cassidy lunch box
pointing my finger
impatiently there—
anywhere opposite.

Light falls on the City of Angels
but it was no angel to you,
enclosed in an orthopedic incrustation, an iron lung.
A daily dose of pills, coral, citron, umber, vermilion,
robin's-egg blue, Russian blue,
Prussian blue, aquamarine.
Wicked and strong.
A drug-peddler's dream.
Expensive!

Grandma choked
on a chicken bone.
She reached into her throat
to pull it out.
Without breath,
life is thin and delicate.

Did Venus rise up in plentitude
from the phosphorus foamy sea?
Did she stand replete with vitality?
Did she force kindness from lust?
Care from trust?
Did she hang neutral in lithium haze
above Disco Bay,
one little twist of the wheel,
one little tap of the foot.

Now Venus in her half-shell hospital gown
sucked her radioactive cocktail down.
She didn't show off her gazelle's neck
or cornflower cape.
No attendants escorted her
to join the other gods.
Just the nurse
with pills
and ether.

The mind is a bow.
The tighter the tension,
the further the arrow flies.
I went and you let me.
Paralysis was your mentor
so you didn't hold me back.
Today is my birthday,
the first without you.
I am almost half a century
and still learning to speak.

On Holt

I am seven years old and Mom has that *No-no!* look
so I talk to the vacant air of the backseat.
The bell that is his mouth rings as Dad turns the wheel
of the Chevrolet singing *Blueberry Hill*,
his black hair shining in the light from the window.
We drive through the valley basin where foothills
catch smog that whisks across our horizon.
We exit the San Bernardino Freeway at Holt Avenue
to our orange grove backyard in Covina.
In childhood I was on hold.
I did not know it, but I was waiting for something
like thunderheads to appear.
Something even like a blizzard or a hurricane
I might step inside to the bottom
and see the cotton trees bend.
I wanted to feel the wind
and maybe fly.

Artie

At the Veterans Hospital on Beacon Hill
Nurse Betty yells at my father's roommate,
Pajama bottoms! Pajama bottoms!
Can't go around this hospital
without pajama bottoms!

My dying father talks about money.
Life without it. Life getting it.
Bane of his life not having it.
What good would it do now?
I see the writing on the wall
was his final cliché,
pronounced under a clock
and *Water Lilies* by Monet.
His last sage advice:
Always cash your checks immediately.

Artie was never pretentious
but impressed by pretense.
His doctor, a Dr. Lord,
flatlined his future.
You're going down that road.
Do you want to avoid it?
Or are you ready to go?
Artie vows to stay alive till
Vargas vs. De La Hoya fight.

On Independence Day
he has a one-night furlough
under the pink vaulted ceiling
of his Soundview condo.

Home for a final sunbath.
To smell the jasmine.
Did he dream of Brooklyn or the Coral Sea?
Did he dream of wife May,
dearly departed before him?

The *lantsman* down the hall
greets Artie on his return from liberty.
What do you have there? he asks.
Lamb chops, Artie says.
But really it was pork loin.

They laid him out in a white sheet
stiff around his ivory body, a totem.
A scrimshaw Eskimo charm
with his perfect teeth set against snow
and his faint sweet death-smell.
I thought he looked free,
let off from his dying chore,
and peaceful, though he hated quiet.

At home, a tiny icon of Archangel Michael,
patron of the sick, soldiers, and policemen,
fell off the shelf when Artie died.
You, angel of insomnia,
disappeared and came back to life.
Is that you washing dishes?
Is it you watching television,
you with your secret loves?
Maybe angels don't make love
they just leave the world
on wings of morphine.

Saint Monica

Some go to church on Sunday or roller-skate the promenade.

Some push shopping carts through vacant lots

in Santa Monica's tennis courts.

The carousel and palm tree clichés.

A blue lifeguard station on pale gold sand.

A silver-haired woman strolls past the sandstone nun,

patroness of marriage and a hard-drinking son.

From her pious tears a Franciscan

named the watery place, Monica,

Latin for advisor,

noona for nun,

and *Monos*, Greek,

for alone.

St. Augustine

He drove a Rolls Royce.

He lived in a castle above Sunset Strip.

Wore Italian suits and was GQ.

He was an optimist, conducted opera,

read history in Lompoc minimum-security.

Like a Tsarina, his mamma ruled with impunity.

He brought her queen's jewels while diddling cloying ladies

in his bubble bath under the glass eyes of Venus.

Friday nights he read the *brucha* by candelabra.

When his mother died, he refused to look at her.

At home, an aquiline starlet descends

a winding staircase her diamond ring a mildew green.

She can't read English, yet Hollywood translates

its message through the neon lips of divorcées

and pompous playboys wrestling sweaty execs

to keep a fig-leaf of respectability.

My GPS doesn't pick up his signal

in hell where the unconscious live.

Back on earth the Graces hold their breaths

in Romanesque swimming pools

under Cypress tree terraces

and heady gardenias.

The Countess

You say what is wrong.
You tell me that you save each day like a button in a box.
Your clothing in the closet hangs without being worn,
Chinese silks, cottons, rough wools with a slight smell of camphor.
This is my introduction to despair. This is my hint
of confusion amongst the minutiae of detail.

I cannot argue with this fact, a condition
that encircles our lives from end to
end as old friends do. Grief is personal and shaped
by circumstances or by stars rotating in the heavens.
The skies are not friendly tonight and the food inedible.

You entered on holidays, Auntie Mame from New York
bearer of gifts from afar. "Doesn't look like a fairy godmother,"
said a kid from our neighborhood as you slept in the foldout bed,
but I knew who you were, my stroke of good luck.
You stroke me, I stroke you.
You are my breath-stroke with mini-strokes.
Flower of Levant, the tulip is yours—
and most beautiful at dying
tinged blue, furled, curled,
sensing light at the windowsill.
Slanted rain streams down the chains

of your forest garden.
You in your loveseat watching birds eat.
A dog at your hearth.
"Everything will be okay," you say.
I liked May's way
of purging the heavy stuff first
and getting cozy later.

At school in Olympia
I was searching Plato's cave
living in my postage stamp
that kept out the night.
Cassandra brought the news
that Grandma was dead.
Drove north on I-5
to Seattle.

The sisters were fighting over
their mother's death.
I was called inside as peacemaker
when I had no peace
nor did I know how to make peace.
I had no phone, no home,
just a car and desire
and you to run to.

But desires are fleeting.
They lose their meaning.
"I want…" trails off an index finger.
Your photographs stare at you
propped on Uzbek pillows
denying the fuss.
So hard to judge how much
love is just enough.

You are the purple thistle fairy
and the red poppy. You touch
the hand-done fine-stitch
to stitch together a multi-
cultural fabric of intellectual chic—
spur me towards my learning streak
where usefulness is no joke
and love for you everlasting.

PART THREE

All Powerful Word

The most reliable thing on earth—sorrow,
And the most enduring—the all-powerful word.

Anna Akhmatova

Utopia

A promise made to yourself that you wished was true.
A lofty distraction necessary for sanity
yet as real as death.
Smells of mortar and brick.
Like "Teen Spirit" onion and spice.
Eucalyptus in a steam bath where
a stranger sings *Los Gardenaias para ti,*
mushroom smells of Plato's Cave
or the familiar smells of home.
It sounds like waves,
cars on the freeway
or bubbling sugar.
You cannot use it as a can opener
or escape in it at will.
It contains all elements
plus blood and bone.
Its intricate architecture
needs constant fine-tuning.
It reminds me of youth
doubles as narrow-mindedness,
exclusivity and fanatical hopes.
It must be colorless or color saturated.
It is not black and white
but limitless, even anarchistic
organized only by nature and not by Marx.
You can't join it. You can't feed it.
You can't preach it or breed it.
Even if I want to believe it
I don't.

In Deep

I

He took me down the cliff and showed me death
how bones are broken
and how the dead don't hurt anymore.
And he told me not to cry, he's *helpless*
and I dried my face to please him.
He wouldn't understand
how a woman turns to the roots of pain
to turn back to the world again.

II

Once, out in the summer of tall California weeds,
the roots of my revolution,
Mr. Job showed us a trapdoor spider spinning her camouflaged door.
How carefully she tended her occupation.
How skillfully she kept her direction
out among the poplars and golden poppy.
Our breathing didn't break her stride.
Our eyes did not inhibit her.

Today, on the cliff, overlooking Fort Worden,
most heavenly place in the Americas,
I can see the regular pulse of the lighthouse
searching steely gray waters.
It shines on a girl in the woods
finding her way along footpaths
picking berries in cowboy boots.
One day she ran into a fox.
She in her Levis, he in fur

and they stared eye to eye
until she got afraid
and he ran off.

III

Standing over Moscow's void in the mud.
These ugly conditions of debris and
dirty spawn defeated Napoleon.
If consideration is not an issue
and eating and pushing forward is,
why even bother with history?
Why keep track of the dead and the living?
Let us yield for the old woman crossing the road
tapping bravely with her wooden cane
for she knows how to walk on ice.

We are all a breath away from mud, from drowning, and from
                falling off balconies.

Where are you tonight?
Is your brain alright?
Still held together with its filaments?
Are you sleeping under the full moon or avoiding its reflection?
Stay hidden. Stay hidden and avoid dogs.
Moscow dogs have no manners.
Manners are not for groomed poodles.
They are signals that keep us from accidents.

Don't want to be your baby.
Don't want to belong to anyone.
Don't want to ride you into town or starve.
Don't want to be pushed by old ladies
in coats buttoned to their chins

or chased out of parks by angry men.
And what comes from the deficits?
I will be with you in this broken ship
and ride through storms till sunrise
but don't tell me not to cry.
It's doing us both a favor.

IV

Afraid of the future, afraid of the past,
finding a way via breadcrumbs to
beat the crows to the trailhead.
Fear of dark spots in the forest.
Fear of unknown space behind me.
Always checking escape routes.
Avoiding mirrors.
Stick to the program.
Intuit a way forward.

The End of Marina Tsvetayeva

On paths of mud you reach your destination. You kiss goodbye your
　　　golden domes.

You press your lips to your children, but they disappear.

A claustrophobic future awaits—an empty house, absence of bells.

Somewhere nearby a bridge is suspended. Beneath it your reflection
　　　blazes.

You wait behind a gate, the iron bars more blessing than a thin
　　　stretched horizon.

Neither your men nor your women contain you.

You wait, the non-action more predictable than your own.

Marina, you climbed a mountain of sorrow with a sadder burden than
　　　Sisyphus.

You were lashed to the helm of a frenetic ship and tortured with
　　　sleeplessness.

When they extracted your tongue from the golden dome, you starved.

All around you the exhausted architecture crumbled.

So you threw yourself into your nomenclature and shut the door

knowing the rope would hold you and welcomed being lost.

Orange Coat

At the trolley stop a woman
with two black eyes wearing an orange coat
lurches across the road.
Where is she going?
She squints to go forward or
is it back?
Empty bottles clink in her bag
as she turns and turns.
Maybe she's lost her way.
Lucky no vehicle hits her
as she decides which way to go.
Trolley surges forward.
Tap of heels getting on, getting off.
Ideology fades away like
an orange coat in the sun.
At home I wear a gray coat
and plunge towards all my lacking.

Perestroika

The train corners over grooves
and we lean as one spine
as if we're one marble sculpture
before it tumbles down.
We lean together as the conductor brakes
skids and clamors through earth
streaming along as one organism past *Mayakovskaya*,
Belorusskaya, Dynamo, Aeroport.
Someone behind me glances over my shoulder
watching me read poetry in English.
I pause mid-sentence.
But no one speaks. No poetry.
Just the crowd heading
where the train leads
straining to hear
the names of stations.

Soviet Women

The newspaper said it was a butcher from Uzbekistan. You could tell as the cuts were so evenly sawed. The three sisters had gathered near the entrance to *Centralni Rynok*, an outdoor market, selling their homemade *smetana,* root vegetables, and tiny dried wild mushroom necklaces strung together with red thread. They carried their homemade goods in plastic checkered bags, the kind you saw all over Europe in the nineties, the bag of the uprooted, the modern equivalent of the battered leather suitcases at the Ellis Island Museum. Sisters from the village with hennaed hair who probably wore flowered dresses with tucked bodices and hems rimmed with rickrack under their autumn jackets. They were still tan from the summer sun after the frozen winter snows that reached their rooftop. The three of them, having sold their goods at the market, spent the night near Sukharevka Metro where I worked at the British law firm Norton Rose typing legal documents for Gazprom Oil Company and for a diamond mine in Irkutsk. I received my paycheck and walked to Gosbank to cash it so that I could take the money to our apartment and hide it in our closet in my Safekeeper Travel Vest with all the secret pockets. I didn't dare leave money in a Russian bank in the nineties. I was walking back to the office, with my scarf tight around my neck, wearing leather boots and gloves. The wind was chill and the ground was gray with caked dirt clinging to the road and walkways. I had to walk studying the ground because it was full of pits and craters, twisted metal, or pipes you could easily trip over. Closer to our office I made a turn from the long low hill of Tverskoy Boulevard onto a side street when I saw them—three decapitated women's heads placed carefully side by side on the sidewalk. They looked like rubber monster Halloween masks you might see at a costume store or like animal heads at a meat market. Took my breath away and when I looked up, I saw a policewoman in the dumpster pulling out a leg. Too late to procrastinate going to the bank. Too late to take the vision back. Too late not to care. Too late to erase their faces from my brain, to un-see. Back at the office I sat next to Svetlana who made me a cup of tea and told me that I would forget.

Poem with Heroes

My first hero was Akhmatova because she endured.
My second was Marina Tsvetayeva because she didn't.
My third was Osip Mandelstam and wife Nadezhda,
her lists of guilty persons and his cockroach poem.
My fourth hero was my mother conflicted by polio.
My fifth a woman whose handshake is limp as a fish.
In her culture women don't shake hands.
My sixth is the filmmaker who sold his own bed
to keep making films.

A helicopter whop-whops through rain and hail.
Crows scream in our neighborhood.
It is morning a few days post-Super Bowl in America
Yesterday's heroes are today's losers.
But what's a loser anyhow?

Akhmatova had nothing to hide.
How did the dictator know her name?
He had a hunter's instinct for game
and stables of artists to show off.
Her knowledge intimidated
as well as her beauty.
Sometimes she waited in line
for an egg, for a name
for any news. And sometimes
she was a loser.

History runs in one door and out the other
without being useful.
And you bang a cooking pot to rid the room of ghosts.
Akhmatova had guests from the past and the future.

My guest comes from the past.
"Does it ever get dark here?" he asks.
He wants to know if he's God.
Meanwhile the jealous gods demand everything
while blonde angels punch me in the arm.
I know that objects in the mirror are closer than they appear.
I realize if I turn the wheel the vehicle turns.
I know after today comes tomorrow.
But sometimes I just want to poke
a stick in an anthill and stir.

Smell of jasmine in light rain.
Pockets of foggy memory.
Messages transferred along electric lines
interfaced with particles from the past.
Rivers of abandoned memorabilia to sort
from a crushing ocean of inertia.

Finally, I'm out on a walk.
At the bottom of the hill I meet a giant
pink-eyed Albino guard dog pacing off-leash.
Too close to turn back so I chase him.
Hydra, you mongrel serpent dog, go back
to your underworld guard duty!
I know about the gates of hell marked *Arbeit Macht Frei*
but you have to die first to enter.
Go back to your post.
You will grow other heads
and become a constellation.

Loyalty is a dog with a bone that won't let go.
After the tug of war and pat on the head,
you make sure there's water in the dish.
Loyalty is passionate but judicious.

Best not expect anything.
When you stop pulling,
the dog might let go.

Jet Lag

I forgot the name of mountains.

I had forgotten English for takeoff

my body rushing before me cruising at 35,000 feet,

my soul 5,000 miles of exhaust behind clinging to memory's thin
 white sheet.

And now I go before myself to arrive cat-like as the plane touches
 down.

Returning is like the horse that gallops forward frame by frame

or the train rising before it disappears.

PART FOUR

Silence as a Crime

I decided it is better to scream. . . Silence is the real crime against humanity.

Nadezhda Mandelstam

Insomnia On Academic Street

A clear window above trolley tracks.
Sane view but incapable of humanity.
I lie down in the background of voices.
The apartment lift goes up and down.
The *Book of Disquiet* is no help.
I am more defensive than the bars
on my hometown windows.

Three A.M.
A child runs across the floor above.
My hair itches. My ear itches. My life itches
and this itch is impossible to reach.
I stare at this tomb of window, this night hatch,
light hatch, escape hatch, death hatch.
I never felt so many possibilities.
My children kept me from jumping.
My typing fingers hold me back.
The future holds me back.
I had to check that scenario
off my list of things to do.

In the dark Moscow hallway
I am careful not to squeak the floor.
It seems the more we eat
the harder it is to disappear.
Soon DNA sets in.
I would like to be fearless of that
as well as black ice.
An ambulance screams past
popping my language bubble.
I could accidently break things
but force myself to be still.
Waiting is an art.

Five A.M. and still awake.
Pillow hot on both sides

wrote the poet from the North
living in decadence and poverty.
The God of Silence stole her voice too,
and turned her to salt just for looking.

I sat in judgment.
Cried in public.
Resisted the confessional
yet keep knocking on that door.
I thumbed through Plato
who was not a casual man.
I know ideals can be poisoned
and are not bulletproof.
When they shatter
a thousand eyes stare back at you.

Don't think about tomorrow.
Picture yourself asleep.
Look at yourself from the outside window.
You share the couch with your love.
You have eaten and your bladder is empty.
For now, forget the slanted snow
and your million reasons for silence.

Reply

Write down that I am an Arab,
that my grandfather's vineyards
were stolen and all the Arab
lands were stolen.

And when I'm left to starve,
I'll eat anything, even the flesh
of those who stole our land.

Mahmoud Darwish from "I.D. Card"

Write down that I am a Jew
from an oppressed people
now known as the oppressor.
Write down that I am a Jew
with brown hair and green eyes.
For all the gold fillings
pulled and piled into mountains,
you are changing the landscape.
Write down that we share the exile stance.
That refugee has always been our name.
That we share holy places
and use the same word for peace.
Write down that I am a Jew in Northwest America,
land of green and dampness,
and I reject the desert, the Promised Land.
I reject that law of both peoples—
An eye for an eye,
a tooth for a tooth.
I'd rather be mute or blind.

Write down that I am a Jew
and I reject the veil, the wig,

and the male god who orders them.
Don't bother with mister, or missus.
No formalities or stalling tactics.
Write that this land belongs to no one.
Only dust claims first ownership.
And over this dust you erect new landscapes.
Over the bones of Abraham,
over the bones of Mohammed's children.
Write down that I reject all your oppressions
and your promised land.
I have walked through the orchards,
those lush landscapes,
and seen tractors roll down
aisles of gleaming fruit.
I've heard the prophets scream
from the rooftops of Jerusalem.
I've heard all the dogmatic arguments
and prayers at the wall.
Yes, write down that I'm a Jew.
Write down that I don't hate anybody.
Write down that I have been angry.
Write down that I have been hungry
but I would rather starve
than eat your flesh.

Oasis

To love you like water.
To reach above mud and sand
or sink in with both feet.
I wanted to bring you daylight
but night gathered your face.
Daylight became background
and no water reached your mouth.

Grief

The Virgin in her naked skin asked God for peace
while breast feeding.
You'll have to wait your turn for blessings, He said,
already not listening.

There are so many slippery slopes. What does that actually mean?
It means when your house slides down a hillside.
It means easy to step on toes and break a foot.
It means complications beyond control.

Oh little town of Bethlehem where
the blind fortuneteller lived with his blind wife.
Perfume cures the Evil Eye, he said
and hopes and fears from all those years
will help change your life.

The wind blows and pine cones become dangerous.
I might have missed the point not delivered by post or media.
Meanwhile, our mogul sits in his A-frame crafting his next golden
                idol
while I try to cross on the green light down on earth.
I am not waiting for messiahs or princes.
I don't want to preach, patronize or collude.

Grief is a short word for a long phenomenon
and is made from pure magma.
Walls cannot stop it.

Implosion

Candle light was available but I want an explosion.
I want concave and parallel lines to collide.
Nothing sensible or brotherhoody.
No peaceful kingdom, safe room, or capitulation.
I want glass to shatter as in the Amos Oz story
of a woman who walked around the kibbutz at night
looking for revenge. She did not understand
why she crushed a plum between her fingers
or pitched the rock that caused the hollow sound of glass.
I know my aggression as an ever present possibility,
a skin I can crawl into. And I will defend and fight
for what my intuition reveals.
I walk through my neighborhood
wearing boots in case of intruders,
discerning intimidations while waiting
for that real-solid-five-star-concept to back hand.
Oh God! No better than a wife beater looking for a victim.
But here is why it's different from that woman with the plum.
I know my abusive self. I set the detonator and watch it blow.
And after the dust settles, I'm sorry,
not in principle, but for the inability
to impart my perceptions.

Who Runs the World?

Sometimes I hear my twenty-eight-year-old voice grasping,
no, I hate the word grasping, she looks for power too
just as other animals do.
Nature doesn't like a grasper, she'd say
in a voice of uncertain certainty searching
for key elements and words as she speaks
like a diver looking for abalone.
It's not just power-trip-female talk
but human in the wilderness
seeking how to proceed.
And if she finds a pearl,
she'd rather not speak.

Sometimes I hear my twenty-eight-year-old voice
in my voice now, toenails on a wooden floor.
Makes me want to run away.
Makes me want to know what she wants.
Is it her meekness that irks me?
Or is it not knowing what to think
but talking anyway,
as children do,
because they
want to run
the world too.

Allow a Little Leeway

(a nautical expression)

Children

They are our friends and our enemies.
They are thieves of time and necessity.
Their children will come along pilfering
genetic bits from our rich pond.
They will never forget the first songs.
Sad for the baby and the pretty little horses.
Now they climb mountains, steer the seas
and calculate grand parkways.
We taught them independence.
They teach us love and forgiveness.
We can't say we lived only for them,
but the longer we live
the more that is true.

Shell

Shell like a vulva,
sea from where it came.
This shell has no feet,
walks on its insides.

Smart Blonde

Standing on the outskirts,
on the edge unable to move forward,
she's already too bright to see.
Of all the heads in the auditorium
hers is the most distinguished, noticeable,
so golden in the gray Northwest light.
Walking down the aisle she disappears in a seat.
She'd like to disappear entirely and
knows how to do this.
How to keep moving. How to be still.
Yet her blond curls give her away.
She pulls them straight but they don't care.
They are electric in any light
and contradict her disappearing act.
She sits near me, her tattered notebook full of scribbles
to be polished into minerals.
Some will be diamonds
but she doesn't care about diamonds.
She's more shell, more rock,
more sea waves pulling from the shore,
her feet feeling the final lap
and foam of Aphrodite's birth.
When she's gone there will be a hole in my heart.
Stalagmites of sharp pain.
The rugged earth does not care
one bit for my tears or hers.
Love is like smallpox.
It stamps you forever like a number from Dachau,

a message in a bottle that says *Help!*
She would never say *save me from this wreck*
but dives down until she finds
the smallest grain of truth.

Czech Fairytale

In Karlovy Vary, we watch kayakers floating downstream
in the humid midday Czech mountain air.
We want to fly like swans but are grounded
by the river and our twin coffin beds.
Don't think of food here, I said when you wanted local cuisine.
In Prague, everywhere we look, the view is more perfect.
Yet we know this is not a fairytale,
though fairytales are made of blood
and Prague is full of the vestiges of wars.
Weaving through crowds on Charles Bridge
we visit the city librarian. You both talk of the homeless
while I envision pup tents amongst the Himalayan
Blackberries and cyclone fences, Seattle's own
pop-up cities beneath our Land of Opportunity freeways.
We watch the sunset from Frank Gehry's *Dancing Houses*.
We, the dancing partners, do not dance.
We are interested in being interested
and walking over cobblestones.
At the castle, overlooking Prague,
we watch the changing of guards and understand
why Kafka felt lorded over and vulnerable as a cockroach.
We look up at St. Vitus' gargoyles
with their tongues hanging out
daring us not to step closer.
We are like that too,
allowing distance
while learning new
walking rhythms.

Ode to My Husband's Back

To his back first seen publically in a photo
taken in a Saint Petersburg apartment
before pink and green rubber tree wallpaper
stained with *Belomorkanal*,
the kind Mayakovsky smoked.
My friends were shocked
when I showed such a back to the public
that covets gorgeous backsides.
His back never turns on me.
It may leave before I do
or move over to make room.
And when far from me, turns
back to me each time
in need to offer his tender
prideful lust.

Hypocrisy

I talk back all the time.
I talk back out loud and silently.
I talk back to the radio.
I'm addicted to the radio.
My addiction started in childhood after hearing
I Want to Hold Your Hand
in bed with an earache in Covina.
In Seattle on lower Queen Anne
I listened to the Watergate Hearings
while hanging corkline on a fishnet.
I listened from Chimacum while
Mckay's cows breathed through my bedroom window.
I wake to NPR, listening from Seattle
or from afar, in Minsk, Prague, or Warsaw,
or at my mother-in-law's in Moscow.
However, liberal media is getting on my nerves
since our current president overturned everything.
I'm happy about the Trump bashing
but disgusted by the Russia bashing.
My mother taught me to clean up my own mess.
Why can't we fix the voting process?
We hack, they hack. The world hacks.
They meddle, we meddle, too.
We just need a scapegoat for the gods to punish
for twisting the truth like they do,
like we never do, of course.
We think our product is better than theirs
and that gives us the right.
I know a lot about hypocrisy.
I'm bugged.
I talk back.
I swear.

Point No Point

Bulky sweater evening.
The Top Side sloshes
with coffee cups and voices,
the regular talk of scores and fish.

I wade down the dock
stacked with dried nets,
disasters of previous nights.

Once we hung a multi-paneled net.
We thought color change confused fish.
But it hung wrong and weak
and confused only us.

The boat smells of varnish, mold, and fumes.
Some men like Playboy,
this one likes charts and tea.

We reverse out of the slip
he hands the wheel to me.
"Head her southeast,
there, where the light blinks,
towards Point No Point."

Tail end of sunset,
silver and salmon pink.
We watch the freighters
pull past shore.
When it's time to lay gear,
we stuff our legs in rolled hip boots,
put on oil skins
stiff with fish scales.

Hydraulic hum
drums over and out
as three hundred fathoms,
three city blocks long,
leave a curtain trail
of bobbing white corks
that slap at the black water.

We shut down to drift.
The stew sizzles.
The oil stove sputters
and the radio squawk begins.

And we wait,
reading books sentence by sentence,
the peaceful slap, lap,
slap, lap, rocking us to sleep.

When the flood tide comes in
we start to pick the net.

The first fish over is a dogfish.
Her tail swings like a pendulum.
I stab her soft belly,
she drips membranes of pups,
and takes hours to die on the deck.
Between us the dripping web reels in
globed with red jellies
that burn barbs in our skin.

A ratfish comes over the drum,
his yellow teeth snap in the mesh.
On his head is a sticky velcro ball
to clamp his female into position.

Seaweed woven through mesh
spills silent on the deck,
green, rust and gold.

The reel rolls with salmon,
glorious silver bullets
with glazed eyes.
The slabs of silver

slide over the drum.

We pick salmon

until the buoy light comes.

In the morning

at the Top Side,

the cook rolls the dice,

says, *Very nice*,

and we roll in our cups with sleep.

Like hookers we talk of the life

and where next to set our nets.

Acknowledgments:

With grateful appreciation for a lifetime of inspiration: Tree Swenson, Sam Hamill, Lee Bassett, Sharon Doubiago, and Paul Hanson.

In recognition of the long dead writers who have sustained me with their words: Anna Akhmatova, Osip and Nadezhda Mandelstam, and Marina Tsvetayeva. A special thank you to Alexander Etkind for *Warped Mourning, Stories of the Undead in the Land of the Unburied*, and to Ed Hogan and Zephyr Press for the translation and publication of *The Complete Poems of Anna Akhmatova*.

Thanks to Andrea Shaffer, Vlad Lanne, and my old writing group: Lamar, Susan, Leone, and Marion. An especially warm deep thank you to Robert Yoder at *Wild Ocean Press*. With endless thanks to my children, Elijah and Shava, for sharing their lives with a writer. To my family: May and Art Albert, Sonia Mitchelson, Marion and Stan Gartler, whose love and encouragement is as essential as breath. And finally to Valeri Ajaja who kept me from the cliffs with love, kindness, humor, brains, and music.

About the Author

Maryna Ajaja was born in 1950 in Los Angeles and has been writing poetry since 1978. She moved to Seattle in 1969 and has also lived in Port Townsend and LaConner, Washington. During the nineties she lived in Moscow and St. Petersburg, Russia. Ajaja is a graduate of Evergreen State College in Olympia, Washington. She has commercially fished in the waters of the Puget Sound, Salish Sea, and in Bristol Bay, Alaska. Since 1997 she has worked for the Seattle International Film Festival (SIFF), and is a Senior Film Programmer specializing in Eastern European, Russian, Central Asian, Baltic and Balkan Cinema. *In Deep* is informed by all the above landscapes and people.